M000316688

My 1st Million Dollars

8 DIGITS ACHIEVED THROUGH: 8 PRINCIPLES OF HIGHLY SUCCESSFUL JET-SETTING MILLIONAIRES

...a heart to heart letter to my younger self...and to you
(if you have your focus on millions).

Dennis Jali

Printed in the United States of America.

ISBN   Paperback   978-1-64361-327-7
        Hardback   978-1-64361-328-4
        eBook   978-1-64361-329-1

Westwood Books Publishing LLC
10389 Almayo Ave, Suite 103
Los Angeles, CA 90064

www.westwoodbookspublishing.com

A heartfelt thank you:

I dedicate this book to God Almighty, for seeing me through every stormy night I had to weather on my path to success, and granting me the privilege to leave a trail for others to follow.

To my life companion on this journey: lovely Amanda, wife of my youth. Sweetheart: every cold night in my life, turned into a fireplace: the day you showed up. Your quiet strength and deep devotion to seeing me succeed is the reason I secretly slip out of bed early in the morning to pursue my dreams.

To my two children: let this book be your constant companion as you too pursue your own dreams using this blueprint of the permanent footsteps dad has left in the concrete for you.

To you dear reader: I commend you for joining me on this journey of reflection as I look back into the corridors of my past, appreciating the lessons and timeless principles I have not only implemented but have come to treasure. Principles in my bag that I brought through into my penthouse across time-zones lifestyle. Here: you can have some of them, 7 in total, let them give you sure footedness as you embark on your own wealth creation journey.

To my hardworking teams both sides of the Equator: without your holding my hands up I would not be flying at the height I am flying now, cruising at the altitudes I am. I thank God daily for your selfless support and dedication. My haters hate you for it. I love and appreciate you all.

Thank you.

Seven Principles: one goal (success)

1. Change your mind.
2. Change your patterns.
3. Change your history.
4. Change what you touch (daily)
5. Change your focus.
6. Change your network (and net-worth).
7. Change your sense of time.
8. Change your assets.

> In life there is nothing static. You are either gravitating towards or away from your goal, period. You are either ringing a till or surrounded by dead silence...or something far worse: drowning in debts.

Dear millionaire to be,

Are you young? It will not stay that way for long. Do you feel old? Then you don't have much time left, to do something. Do you have your eyes locked on your first million dollars? You are not the only one. Do you have your eyes locked tight on your first million dollars for real? What else are your eyes locked on? Your habits perhaps? I hope that is the case. For your sake I do. It's your habits, the people around you, your choices and ultimately thoughts and actions that will determine whether you are gravitating towards or away from that million.

In life there is nothing static. You are either gravitating towards or away from your goal, period. You are either ringing a till or surrounded by dead silence...or something far worse: debts. What is it for you? Towards or away. It's easy to tell: is your till ringing or silent? Is it coins or notes? Is it constant or far in-between? You have probably watched a shopkeeper own a till, and thought tills belong in shops. Certainly not. If you had a till that you owned and rang it each time money came into your life: you will be shocked how alert you suddenly become. How aware of transactions you become. Most importantly how aware you become of the silent moments in between.

What sound are you hearing right now? What picture do you have in your mind right now? Let me put one forward: a sound of a till ringing consistently. The sight of a till begging you to cash-up because it cannot contain your cash anymore, it's time to make room: you have exceeded your own targets. You have checked out all the boxes you have set for yourself.

Welcome to the world of possibilities. Say goodbye to your days of waiting on the government to come rescue you. Here's what you can know for sure the government is coming for, when you see them advancing in your direction: your taxes, if you have and income and your vote, if you have a heart-beat, still.

Outside that: everything else the government gives you is not promised, nor guaranteed. The very free ways they gave you, are not free after all. Have you seen the levels of government debts piling up? Ask the International Monitory Fund. The last the government wants to do is come and free you, they are busy freeing themselves out of the cob web of debts they have made over the years. Monetary and otherwise. Military debts from the pact they signed and now they owe their 'brotherhood' out there something. Be grateful for what they do, but that's just about it, don't expect much.

Get out there and find the necessary stuff that will begin to ring your till. You don't have a till? You don't have a hustle? Build one. Find one. But whatever you do: get on with it. Don't just sit there.

I have a gentle warning for you: whilst you are at it. You may want to put this book down if you are not going to give a serious ponder to the heart to heart advise enclosed in it. You only have about 70 years or so to be on this earth: you do not want to waste it being broke. What's worse than being broke? Reading a book whose contents you are not going to implement. Taking advice that you are not going to take to heart or do something about. I was born among rats, but today I live among kings of Wall Street. I was born to domestic worker parents, but today my money works for me domestically here in the US and off-shore, and yes: my domestic flights are fast becoming a private jet standard.

If that is worth anything to you: you may want to pause and listen to what I have to say. You may want to put this book down or best yet: throw it in the trash right now or go ask for your refund from the book store, or did you get it from Amazon? I am sure Jeff's team would not mind you stepping forward and pleading that your money was wasted. They will probably refund you. But whatever you do don't waste your time. There is no refund for that.

Why do you want to make your first million dollars? I don't know, and I don't need to, it's irrelevant at this stage. Let big brother, a man born on the southern tip of a continent called Africa, you call it the mother land? Yes that part of the world: and outlived every curve ball poverty threw at me, let me share with you a thing or two about your realising your million dollar ambition.

A thing or two: okay why don't you make it 7things or 8 things? Eight habits I have come to cultivate and respect. The eight things that I have come to perfect, in order to come within grasp distance of a million dollars.

You better listen carefully. Because some of these stuff you have heard before. It's like the law of gravity: it affects every single one of the eight billion human beings on this planet. These stuff is universal. At some point you caught a glimpse of these habits. Whether through your distant rich uncle, or through Hollywood's movie scene, or through a book you half read – just don't half read this one, and don't even scan it, take it to heart, interrogate it and implement it – it might just be your best eight step journey you have taken.

In their race to put a man on the moon: both Russia and America had to fight the same gravitational pull to navigate the earth's barrier. So before you think of yourself smart, or perhaps too smart: learn from me, because I also learnt form the greats. Men and women placed on my path that shaped my thoughts. Men and women who recalibrated my expectations. From Africa's Durban coast to Miami's beaches, to New York's signature street, yes Wall Street, to the streets of London, I bumped into like-minded men and women who pursued wealth with a single minded purpose to beat the odds.

Men and women who had to navigate bad habits they inherited, by default from others, to get to a point where they had to form healthy habits. Habits of giants, industry giants. Habits that changed the magnetic energy and pull in their life. Habits that moved them towards the light and away from the darkness that had come to define their lives, the sad sorry lives they had come to know and accept, towards fresh possibilities.

Did you see that right there? Habits don't just form all by themselves. They require your buy in, your active action. They require your careful thought. Most importantly, they require something God blessed you with: the gift of free will. The will to choose. You have it. How are you going to use it? Will you choose poverty or success? Will you choose success or excuses? Will you choose users or those who will push you towards your destiny? Will you choose brave company or a company of losers?

Will you choose healthy habits or poisonous ones? Let me pause for a moment and share this: I was born in the heart of South Africa's KwaZulu Natal, in Botha's Hill, a place west of Durban. A place sprawling with hills and valleys. Where you chose to build pretty much determined the view you will wake up to in the morning.

That view you wake up to by default determined what type of day you had. Let me put it practically: if you build your hut in the valley, you were bound to lose a certain amount of sunlight.

The sun would be delayed by up to three hours or more before it emerges in your window, if you chose to dwell in the valley. That's your address my brother or my sister. You chose that piece of real estate. You probably went to a local iNduna, also known as a tribal chief and asked for that piece of land, sometimes through ugologo – a gift of alcohol – but nonetheless that will be your portion for years to come.

6

Who knows: maybe that will be your family's home for at least generations to come. Children will be born and later will die, calling that place their home, because you chose it. By default of choosing to live in that poor community, in that poor part of the community, and in the valley area of that community, you have certain things that will take place by default because you made your choice. You exercised free will. That's just how powerful choices are.

Did I mention: that valley dwellers have a sunset much earlier than most of us? Their sun sets hours earlier than most of us. In economic terms: if there's recession, they get to feel it first. They get hit first.

Before I expand for you on the legendary life of mountain dwellers I can almost hear you thinking, but Mr Jali: what about slavery, what about apartheid and what about forces against me, forces I cannot control.

That, young man or young woman is not what this book is about. That's not what this letter is about. This is about the 99 percent forces that you do have control over. The habits you can observe and form in your life.

Habits that once you form them: they will begin to form you, whether you realise it or not. You form habits then you are asked by life: to vacate the director's chair and watch as an audience, as your habits begin to form you.

When I chose to leave KwaZulu Natal rural, the country side, and go to the BIG city of Durban, I made a choice. When I chose to enrol in that Chef school, I made a choice. When I chose to accept a menial job in once of Durban's oldest hotel, which ones became a hotel of choice for Her Majesty The Queen of England, Durban's Royal Hotel. I made a choice. A string of choices that would later bring me in the vicinity of a trade that has come to define me. The international trade in foreign currency. When I left the hotel that faithful day and chose to go to the Internet café during my lunch break, instead of heading for the canteen: I made a choice. Is it not amazing to you how a choice, then another, can be like a string of actions that mimic a child putting one foot in front of the other as they hold onto a couch, and suddenly they have dashed across the lounge.

I have three children with my wife. The wife of my youth, and we have watched them grow into bright cute children. It was not without it's moments. I watched them crawl. I watched them fall on their butts. I watched them refuse to make excuses, I watched them get up from the floor each time they fell. They did not get the memo, that iIF YOU FALL IT DEFINES WHO YOU ARE. They did not get the memo that if you do not achieve your goals the first time around then quit. See: none of the eight habits I am about to share with you include quitting.

Remember that picture of valley dwellers in the village? You thought I was not going to go back there right? I hate to disappoint you. Which side of the neighbourhood are you from: The Bronx or Brooklyn? The East Coast or Texas London, Maryland Nigeria or Abuja? You and I have something in common. Let me prove it to you.

See: when you pick a mountain as your address. A place upon which you will pitch your eight bedroom, your shack or your mud-hut, something happens: fresh possibilities are born, out of that choice. By the time you put this letter down: I would love for you to have a new appreciation for choices, habits and patterns.

Patterns are everywhere. Look up right now, the ceiling above you has a pattern. Pick up a leaf: there is a pattern to it. Even your DNA has a pattern to it. A mastery that cannot be copied or duplicated. So if you admit, as crime thrillers and science have proven so many times: that the human DNA is one of the most fascinating inventions by God and discoveries by humans: then why would you doubt that success has a gene and a DNA to it. A pattern you can detect, appreciate and begin to weave it into your own life. Pay careful attention because I am sharing my pattern and weave method, if you do what I do, you will get similar results, no matter your field of choice, talent or trade discipline. Success is success. Success breeds success. Money is green. Your money is as green as everyone else's.

Ask Siri: she will tell you the stuff she has been observing about your driving patterns, your voice signature, your choice of websites, your social media tool of choice, your most frequently used contacts – that is your real inner circle right there – your preferred routes home and to work or the office, your type of digits you usually work out in your calculator, the types of mails you send, the level of conversations you hold, the depth of humour you appreciate, your waking and sleeping patterns, what time you wake up and what time you dose off. See: Siri has been observing you, a lot closely than you realise. If you were to interview her, she will reveal to you more about your habits than you yourself realised.

If Siri can do that: what about you? Why can't you do that? Why can't you observe your own life? Why can't you observe others? Why can't you for once ask yourself: who is out of my league? Why are they out of my league? Most importantly: is that the league I want to be in? Do I have an excuse not to be in that league? What barriers to have to surmount to be in that league? Am I willing to pay the price to be in that league? Put in every effort required of me? Watch yourself closely: catch yourself practicing good habits, yes you have them. And in the same token catch yourself practising bad habits. The kind of habits that do not build you, but are busy tearing you apart.

Why do you spend four hours a day on social media? What are you doing in there? When you add three hours of tv or video games, or just hanging out, you soon find that you are throwing your life down the rat hole. Did you add up how many days your social media habits amount to? I dare you to whip out that calculator and ask yourself, add up the numbers.

Back to that address on the hill: it is the peak of the village. You see the sun first as it comes up marching like a warrior into the picture, greeting you with a constant unfailing smile. And yes: you will be among the last human beings to bid the sun farewell before it calls it a day. How is that? Your choice of real estate in the heart of South Africa gives you privileges valley dwellers do not have. They made their bed right: now they are lying in it.

Before you jump to their defence, and scream: by big brother these people were born under oppression. The last time I checked: both America and South Africa are more imbued with opportunities now more than ever before. It's all around you. But it won't come knocking, you will have to go looking for it. Here is what I found the hard way: there is an expiry date to every lie and excuse you have ever told yourself as to why you are not successful yet. As to why you have not yet held that million dollar bank balance slip as yet or wake up in that address of choice. Perhaps today it is the oppressor who did not let you have that house. But one day you wake up and realise: the oppressor is long gone, at least the original oppressor. The only oppressor that remains is...wait for it: you. Through the lies and excuses you cling onto. Through your wait for the government to come through.

See: that trip to the Internet café that day, when I skipped lunch to find out about this crazy thing called Forex, I stepped into a realm of possibilities that was not available to me until that moment. A realm of transactions my own grandfather had never dreamt of. A realm of creating wealth that was and remains out of reach to many. Yes: this trade has its risks, medicine has its risks as a procession. When I open a trade, I bring every level of expertise known to me at that point I bring a hawk eye level of astute diligence to that graph movement, but ultimately I have to navigate risks just like you navigate risks through traffic on your way to work.

I remember seating back and hearing the story of this one brother I admire: Tyler Perry, how he had to navigate tough circumstances growing up. I had it hard growing up, back in KZN, South Africa, so naturally, his story gripped me. How he had to jump over graves on his way to school, drug neighbourhoods and the busiest of intersections on his way to school. But education meant something to him, something dear to his heart, that he was willing to jump the gauntlet and make to school and back. Look at him today, he owns a 230 million USD jet, that's my kind of resilience. That's my kind of life: not without its risks, but the reward tend to remind you that the climb uphill was certainly worth every ounce of your strength. And worth every dollar you invested. Every right decision you made. Every right relationship you invested in. Every great contact you stored on your phone. Every right turn you took, and every bend you negotiated at the right speed, and every time you kept to the speed limit. It all adds up doesn't it?

It's time to bring that level of consciousness to this thing called wealth. Have you driven a motor vehicle before? Have you noticed how observing other driver's behaviour improves yours?

So read further as you learn and observe the eight habits of highly successful millionaires. It's only eight of them. I know there's a lot, but if you appreciate numbers like I do you will know that there is a significance to the number eight, signifies a new beginning or resurrection. Apart from that: it's a neat number, saves both of us time.

Before I start, guess what: if I was to write a letter to me at 16. A letter to that young desperate, confused, hopeless, broke self, it will be this one. So in a way, that boy back then, the boy I used to be is joining you as you read on. You are in great company, a company of someone that was more frightened than you, more full of excuses than you, made more mistakes than I care to count, and yet: perhaps more resilient. Are you resilient, bold and want to make something of your life? Then you have something in common with the younger me, that's where I started, right there. Raw guts, then the knowledge and 'learning how to walk' followed from there on. Lots of head bumps, I will save you those, but nonetheless I pushed through, despite odds.

Here we go: let's start from the beginning, move through scenarios and work ourselves to those habits, thoughts and actions of the greats. Actions that continue to reform my life daily. Habits that continue to define me to this day. Habits I have in common with some great successful souls on this planet. Men and women that refused to take a no for an answered: stared at the odds and demolished past every excuse.

Realise this: one of the greatest mistake as mankind is the refusal of the principle of sowing and reaping. Governments, organizations, corporations, institutions and families use fewer rewards and appreciation methods to create sustainable economy. Companies and corporations are less likely to create these systems where majority of their clientele could take up to 30% of profits generated through their network while maintaining a sustainable growth for all stakeholders. This creates scarcity and produces more desperate economies with less people willing to participate in those due to lack of money circulation. To paint a clear picture:

Let us say Tom is one of the 5 community members works for company A, lives in Area C right next to Shop Z (remember that till we discussed) which sells everything from food to toys. The cost of living rises up by 10% a year and companies usually give their employees a 15% raise per annum. Company A decides not increase Toms salary for two years. This results in Tom not being able to keep up with the ever increasing cost of living. Not only that but it has also made Tom to carefully choose how he spends his last dime. Unlike before he now only goes to Shop Z once in two weeks buys selected items for his survival and spend zero dollars on entertainment. Tom moves out of area C.

The chain reaction to this is that Area C has now an apartment empty because Tom moved out and it has affected the landlord who barely has enough to pay for it himself unless he finds a tenant soon. Because the landlord now has to pay the institution on time to keep afloat. Looking at this apartment he decides he will lessen his personal needs and pay the mortgage till a new tenants moves in. Furthermore Shop Z owner decided to shut down their entertainment department because there not enough customers and this results in suppliers of the entertainment units having to close down their operations.

This chain reaction happens daily. When an entrepreneur decides to take a step of faith jump into business there are just two options. Make it work and everybody enjoy the success and impact peoples' lives positively or Fail and lose your business and everybody pays for it even those who weren't directly involved in your business. See how the landlord is paying a price for Company A? You could be somebody else's victim because they never set up that Business or made that call, Just like the landlord is victim of their decision not to increase Tom's salary? You have to position yourself today not wait today. This book – or you can see it as an open letter to you - is designed to get your to your best position in this economy and how to swim while others sink in this economy. How to create a wealthy you and successful you in every situation. Follow our pattern and you will learn that and harness that know-how.

First and foremost, it is very important as a first step towards financial liberation that you:

Discover where you are financially:

I am not certain how far you went with your observation of the philosophers from years gone by. But there was a man called Socrates: he once said "a life not examined is not worth living". Let that sink in a bit. Let your antennas be lit. Let that awareness sink in further as you begin to examine your life, an honest heart to heart right there. Where are you financially today?

Most people have no sense of where exactly they are in this economy. They just have jobs, they just have stock just have investment, but there is no real goal and without a goal or big picture in mind, then it does not matter if they achieve anything financially or otherwise, for as long as bills are paid. That is futile. That till we spoke about must ring. But there must be purpose to that till ringing. A purpose bigger than your stomach's needs. A purpose bigger than your rent that is due this month end. A purpose that will outlive you. A beyond pay cheque to pay cheque existence.

I have come to realise, soberly so, that there are three levels you will accordingly find yourself in, somehow.

I am not certain how far you went with your observation of the philosophers from years gone by. But there was a man called Socrates: he once said "a life not examined is not worth living". Let that sink in a bit. Let your antennas be lit. Let that awareness sink in further as you begin to examine your life, an honest heart to heart right there. Where are you financially today?

The first level you will most likely find yourself:

1. Ground Zero:

This is the level where unfortunately most people are. It's quite a popular position to find yourself in on the financial spectrum. Neither rich nor poor. They barely pay their debts but at least they pay them and the rest is history. They networth is still zero after all the debts are paid. They have no real assets things can bring them fortunes overtime. They have a tendency to think that the grass is greener on the other side till they get there. They never want to fix what wrong here but they move other there so easily. They quit everything they start. They usual hate to be responsible for others. They want to be safe. The safest place I know is maximum security prison and they usual end up locked in their own made financial prison.

2. Debts:

This group or financial position where most discover that if they would stop working even for a month or two or three: they would most likely lose their home, or their car, or access to education and all the work they have done over the years is to dig themselves deep into the hole. Some have really deep that it looks like there is no hope in their perspective since all they had hoped for had landed them right into their financial nightmares. Some may have taken some risk in the past but only for the wrong reason. They do not take risk, nor possess an appetite for it. Low or high risk, such a threshold is just not there in their DNA or social or moral fibres that make up their proverbial genetic make-up or inform their daily set of choices and life routines as they 'do life'. They pay too much attention on what they have lost or could lose as opposed to what they could gain.

3. Credit (as in credit worthiness)

This is the oil of the engine or what one can refer to as the cream of the crop. They keep their lamp burning for years and it will not run dry. They are the reason there is still hope for many for their approach is not only to build for today but with the long term in mind. Such forms the theme of their daily grind in all they do. Whenever they transact they say to themselves: if I buy this how will this affect my overall performance. They reward themselves constantly to achieve more even with what appears to be less. They invest in others and they follow their own intuition. By so doing they master their own life by following the intuitive voice which is more clear and loud than the voices outside. They believe that success is possible.

All they have to do from there onwards is repeat a learnt pattern to achieve millions and down the road if they stick to that, their millions turn to billions. Since they were able to turn hundreds to thousands and thousands to millions. So for you to measure your current position financially you will need to take a test.

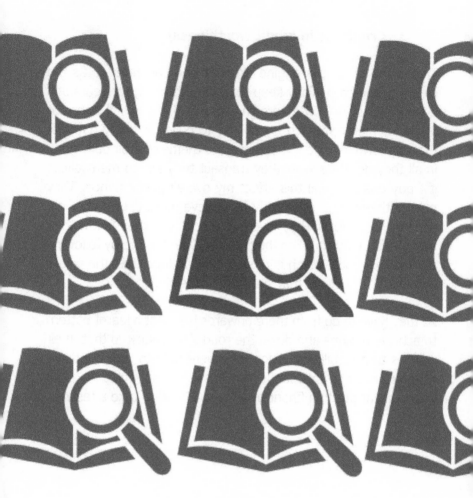

"All they have to do from there onwards is repeat a learnt pattern to achieve millions and down the road if they stick to that, their millions turn to billions. Since they were able to turn hundreds to thousands and thousands to millions. So for you to measure your current position financially you will need to take a test."

Simply write down all answers to following questions.

Assets & Liabilities

Totals:

- How much are your assets worth: _____
- How much are your derivatives: _____
- How much is your network worth: _____
- How much are your liabilities: _____

What does the above picture tell you? Ponder on it a bit.

Once you see the above picture, it will probably spur you into action. Action is what triggers momentum, towards your destiny. What are you waiting for? It's time to start climbing out of the reality you do not want towards a reality you do want and desire.

Action Time [Formulate a Plan]:

Discovering where you are financially won't solve the problem but at least you know how hard you have to work and what needs to be changed. With the curriculum we have put together below, think of it as a road map, to help you take steps into the future. Following our proven pattern will give you a proper tracking towards your future. Our 8 steps guideline is based on these three principles. Remember those habits? They are born out of principles, your value core, instil that, you are in motion.

Someone once told me: to clean an entire house, first start by making the bed, you will feel like half of the job is as good as done. So where should you start, now that you have this level of awareness in your finances?

Start here:

Change your mind:

A significant shift or lasting transformation in life first begins via a significant shift in your mentality. Embracing this reality will contribute to more than half your success, its half the battle won.

This is a real game changer, if you were to truly embrace this foundation principle of them all, when it comes to success and wealth creation. This means that sum choices of one's life especially in the area of finance is subject to their view, mindset and influences around them and is a reflection of everything that is known or ignored by them and change in any of these things will result in change in expenditure and result in change in behaviour leading to wealth or gains.

Proceed with:

Change your patterns:

In life there's this thing called a pattern. Even before business sense (connecting dots in business), an awareness of patterns will become your invisible weapon aligning you for success.

The idea that one's misfortune has nothing to with their past actions or their future gains will have nothing to do with today is the distorted image of the truth. This is nothing but a lack of true faith that leads to action. Life moves in patterns and trends. Once you realise that and actively formulate habits with this in mind, those habits take over your life, becomes your character and your character will give you your destiny.

Fashion, patterns or trends happen daily. We just have to decisively choose what trends we formulate today based on the outcome we seek to have. Just a like civilian can start a habit of drug use and alcohol abuse till they are completely submerged under the control of the substance the same thing can be done with one's future. You can let your future control you now just by starting a habit today.

Then:

Change your history:

Wisdom dictates that if we are to understand our future, or have a clue about what is on the horizon, we do best to reflect on our past. Time to reflect.

Did I hear you say: you cannot change your past? Well if you begin to reflect on what went on back then, you will begin to actively avoid history from repeating itself. Get in there and begin editing your future, by first understanding the why in your existing past.

Pick up any good psychology material, you will soon find a common pattern in accepted logic that in life in general Human psychology has proven to have progressed so little over time. It takes time for people to break off the cycles they are going under. People who have bad relationship are more likely to suffer and be victims more than one time, People who loses money usual have had many experiences in this subject and so are people who are successful. They can tell you story after story of how they made money investing in this and then this and then that until you starting they have luck and those loosing have bad luck but in truth all that is happening is constantly the life cycles that came with the habits keep coming back and the victims keep making the same mistake and the victorious ones keep doing what is right and winning. This is where we help you realize what you believe about yourself and see opportunities when they come knocking at your door and seize the moment.

History tending to repeat itself means you will get another Opportunity down the road, but what are going to do this time that is different from the last time? That is the question to ask yourself.

If a dog can form a habit so can a human being. After some training and workshop you will have new habits and you can rest assured success is yours for the taking. The evaluation of choices and opportunity costs is subjective; such evaluations differ across individuals and societies.

To unleash your full Potential, before reading the next portion do the following:

- Make an effort to practice all you learn in each chapter
- Look around you and write down 2 things you can have.
(buildings, cars, assets etc anything you see name it)

_____

_____

- Look around you write down things that are for your benefit and for your gains.
(for example the road is for you travels to fro. Beneficial things to you and your dream)

_____

_____

_____

_____

_____

- Close your eyes and count to 15 while you are only thinking about assets. What did you see?

_____

_____

- Write down 8 things that would change if you owned the assets you want to own.

_____

_____

_____

- Write down one thing you can do to get you closer to your goal:

_____

- Write down 1 act of celebration & 1 gratitude acts

_____

_____

Remember: life changes when we learn new ideas. Embrace these ideas.

"" A Goal in mind is defined as the final milestone you want to reach or the final picture you want to see or results you want to realise: in your personal life, career or ministry, or in any area of your life. The best way to advance towards your goal is to lay a foundation and by dreaming, not dreaming in your sleep, but envisioning results you desire. It's time to brush the dust off your vision board. ""

Let's drill this definition down to its basic granular level:

A Goal in mind is defined as the final milestone you want to reach or the final picture you want to see or results you want to realise: in your personal life, career or ministry, or in any area of your life. The best way to advance towards your goal is to lay a foundation and by dreaming, not dreaming in your sleep, but envisioning results you desire. It's time to brush the dust off your vision board.

We have to dream because dreams do come true. We have to believe it and follow through and be excited about it. The bible says unless we become like children we would not inherit the kingdom of God. Being childlike is different from being childish. We have to go back to our original source of harvest and that source of harvest is in the dreaming. Men and Women who have walked upon the earth and changed the course of mankind did it by simply allowing their dreams to lead them, From Abraham to David and Daniel to our Modern day Martin Luther King Jr, Nelson Mandela to Benson Idahossa, all these men have something in common. The dreamed and they all individually believed nothing else but their own dreams. They followed through and they were decisive.

They refused to follow societies dictatorship of how their Life should be. Set a time every day to sit and ponder on your dreams, remind yourself of all the prophecies that may have been spoken to you or words of inspiration about the future. This will help create a stronger healthier belief system about yourself. Remember you have to be like a child. This also means you have to be happy 80% of the time and avoid worrying! It does not solve anything, quit trying it does not get anything done, just do not worry! So go ahead start today dream on for dreams will come true. Yours too, from time to time stop and ponder and dream for you shall be rewarded greatly. Your dream will come true. This book maybe just the beginning of your success.

Prepare yourself for the journey. Most people cannot dance but when the music is on and they start to move to the rhythm. It will soon look like they are dancing. Yes they will be regarded as dancers etc but all they did is find the rhythm and find the tune. The rest is history.

The same principle applies in your life. Once you find the rhythm of success and it aligns with your dream then you would have been aligned with great stars of the world and your life will change for the better. Rhythm is basically your pace, in tune with your reality. Your consistency in following through. People who won the lottery in this world are still not successful. It also helps get you out of tune towards negative influence as you know you cannot dance to two rhythms at the same time.

Lock your sights on that end goal

It was Daisaku Ikeda who boldly declared: I believe that we must maintain pride in the knowledge that the actions we take, based on our own decisions and choices as individuals, link directly to the magnificent challenge of transforming human history [starting with our own]

This is a must:

Change what you touch:

Wisdom dictates that if we are to understand our future, or have a clue about what is on the horizon, we do best to reflect on our past. Time to reflect.

You want success. Starting by touching it. Move away from fiddling with that which does not look or feel like success. Touch success. The things that you touch every day can help create belief e.g. your Phone. Imagine that every time you touched your phone it was because of some good news from your businesses. Every time you touch phone pause for a three seconds and think about how that will make you feel and all the phone calls coming are only bringing good news and success.

To create this pattern you need to have reminders of who You are becoming every day. Put pictures and visual boards where you will see them effortlessly, play music and listen to messages that line up with your goal. Wear clothes that speak to you and about who you are. Success is an idea that translate to something we can touch and see and smell every day. It is not a idea based on greed but it is based on convenience, liberty, and choices we make. You have to make people see what choices you have made even through your personal appearance. Your office and your home have to speak for themselves. Not forgetting your smile.

How about that firm handshake and a non-hesitant decisive yes. You are making a big choice here you are choosing success or failure and the rest will be history Success has to be chosen. The choice goes across all institutions such as the nation itself, families, churches, organizations, businesses and at an individual level still.

The success of one person has an influence over at least a 1000 people, at least within the same nation. So is the failure of one man, it can affect that one person but ultimately it can affect thousands of others who may never get to change their lives because someone in their chain failed to ignite the flame and so the whole group remained in darkness.

Just remember the story of Tom that we discussed previously. It happens every day. To paint a better picture let me talk about myself. Remember what I mentioned before, about being born in South Africa during the apartheid system. It seemed like a crime to be black and demand freedom for the country, because of this many people spent years in prison, protesting the government of moving from province to another, when the system of apartheid was overthrown and rebound for the black man to re-establish the nation.

The more I think about it: the South African government should have done a full study of what it was going to take to rebuild the nation and what impact the apartheid had had on everyone. When the apartheid was over guess what was not over? The chain reaction of poverty was not over, especially the deeply entrenched system of thinking and inherently bad choices and patterns. Since my mom could not go and study where she would, she ended up working for families in the city, since we did not live with her we lived with our grandmother, since we could not attend the best schools because she could not afford that we ended going to whatever school that was in the area, since those schools did not have the resources then our level of education was affected greatly and so for forth and so forth!

A chain reaction was formed. A pattern that had to be broken, one way or the other. The result of this chain reaction was a lot of broken dreams and lot of unfulfilled wishes. But I made a choice. I refused to believe that I was going to end up in poverty or that kind of misery. I was not going to end in that shabby place. My choice was made and here I am today.

Some reflection time:

What chain reactions do you want broken from your life?

_____

_____

_____

_____

What steps will you take to break it?

_____

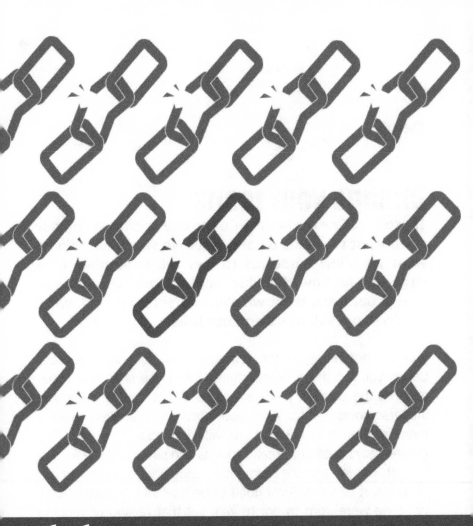

My mother could not afford good schooling for us. We ended going to whatever school that was in the area. Since those schools did not have good resources then our level of education was affected greatly and so for forth and so forth. **A chain reaction was formed...a pattern that had to be broken**, one way or the other. The result of this chain reaction was a lot of broken dreams and lot of unfulfilled wishes. But I made a choice. I refused to believe that I was going to end up in poverty or that kind of misery.

Then this:

Change your focus:

Those first few moments into the day upon opening our eyes, what we focus on and what we see in our minds, what we allow ourselves to feel will determine, to a large extend how that day will turn out. The same is true of our lives. What we allow ourselves to feel, what we dwell on, will transform our lives.

You are not ready, in the remotest way, to handle success unless you get this principle right. Unless you shift your focus towards the success you want to have. Let that be what you immerse yourself into. What you touch and feel every waking moment. Touch that dream. It will draw closer to you. The greatest joys in all our breakthroughs and success is the feeling we get, the joy and the moment of celebration that comes out of these. It certainly feels good to be a winner, because that's what we were born to do: to win. Let that feeling of winning invigorate you.

Does the thought of winning make you smile? That means you are feeling it already. A significant shift or lasting transformation in life first begins with a significant shift in your mentality and what you allow your senses to dwell on. Let that winning moment come alive. Hear that till, see yourself holding that bank slip with digits almost feeling the bottom of the paper, or your mobile device if you are on online banking. Embracing this reality will significantly proper you towards your victory, your dreams and ultimately your destiny. The reality you want.

Let me share a story. I am not even certain if this movie is available on Netflix now, given how old it is. It's called: Chariots of fire. When it comes to holding onto deep convictions in your heart, this movie displays that quite strongly.

A bit of background: Chariots of Fire is a 1981 British historical drama film. It tells the fact-based story of two athletes in the 1924 Olympics: Eric Liddell, a devout Scottish Christian who runs for the glory of God, and Harold Abrahams, an English Jew who runs to overcome prejudice. He refused to run on a Sabbath as he wanted to honour God by observing the Sabbath instead of running. This bold decision becomes as flagship moment in Olympic history.

Something else is worth noting in this piece of history. The importance of feeling. See what Eric Liddell said: I believe God made me for a purpose, but he also made me fast. And when I run I feel his pleasure. He added: you can glorify God by peeling a potato if you peel it to perfection. Feel it, perfect it. Victory will precipitate.

About your focus. Despite the anti-Semitism opposition he experienced, Eric Liddell focused on God and his God-given purpose. He focused on the breeze he felt on his face, and the wind that was carrying him to victory as he bolted towards the finish line, not the jeers of haters. Do you have haters? Soak in the feeling of victories awaiting you, not the stinging words of haters. As the gun fired, to signal the start of the race, Eric refined his focus, and fixated himself on the feeling of victory awaiting him. Do the same.

What you start feeling from the moment you wake up each day is critical and yes you can and you must choose your feelings carefully. Your brain is able generate joy from what you meditate and think about but this time take 5minutes and think about how you will feel when all your dreams

Your brain is able generate joy from what you meditate and think about. Meditating can require as little as 5 minutes. Block at least five minutes and use this time window to think about how you will feel when all your dreams are achieved. Does it make you smile? That means you are feeling it already. Stay in it as longs you can. Most people are busy searching for joy but they do not realise that you can have joy once you have the right belief system. This is quite a significant revelation.

Remember how we dwelt on the power of choices earlier? Take note of this: feelings are a choice too. You can chose how to feel. This maybe a difficult one for many but this is where discipline needs to take place. How you feel is not just based on what happened but it is based on what you think about what happened. Again your processing of information is a big factor between your hopes and your sadness.

You can choose to happy about what you believe is coming your way now while maintain a level of reality. You don't deny the reality you just cannot let it dictate your fate. Your personal understanding is that with or without your reality your success is guaranteed because it is not based on someone or something is steadily based on your habits and your character. This means that if you don't become a millionaire this way you surely going to become one another way either way you will become one.

This has to be your belief system built in within you. It's not important what others say about you more than what you say about yourself. This book is more powerful when you read it and believe for yourself because it helps you build those component you will need for the next level.

I felt rich long time ago so I started giving away my little Dollars to churches. I did not even have a $1000 but I knew what I felt was based on my habit. Over the years habit will start to tell you where you are going and they leave no doubt. Every criminal who has formulated a habit they have their habit speaking to them justice will catch up with you one way or the other. The longer you keep your habit the harder it is to break them. Man can you imagine what it's like for me to live this life knowing this secret? No wonder I'm always trying to help someone or some church, I love it cause I can never run dry I know The Source. Those who know their source can never run dry. Feel it today don't just drag yourself out of bed but rise up and form a habit yes do it again. Start your day the right way. I never leave the house if my wife and I are not right with each other because if I do I will take that habit for that day with me to my next meeting so I wait and sort it out because I like to win. Being good is part of my winning and it should be part of your winning too. This means that I'm focusing not on whether I'm right or she is wrong

I'm focusing on restoring peace and that means sometimes I have to swallow my pride because peace is better than being right. Some people don't enjoy being good! They don't know what good for good! And they don't know how good it is to be good. Yes this helps maintain a balance a certain level of joy in your heart and peace and I am telling you nothing brings a greater winning secret that tranquillity.

Some cats and dogs be fighting while the rat is nibbling away at the cheese. If you are good then your goodness should be so good that wrongs just dies or shrinks in your presence, bring peace and joy to your office, work or home. Let your presence be felt because you invest enough in your feelings not just for the moment for but for your character. Remember: your success will inspire many, well beyond your time here on earth, many beyond your immediate reach or realisation.

> Man can you imagine what it's like for me to live this life knowing this secret? No wonder I'm always trying to help someone or some church, I love it cause I can never run dry I know The Source. Those who know their source can never run dry. Knowing this secret will translate into the law of abundance operating in your life. The secret to life is in giving, sharing and that is how you multiply what you have, through generosity.

This is critical:

Change your network:

In the same way money has a language to it, and how success has or requires a certain posture before you attain it: success also has an aroma to it. This of it more as coffee. Success has its own coffee beans to it, it's time to wake up to that aroma of success if you are going to sip on that success called wealth.

If something smells like a failure a mile away, guess what: it probably is failure. Trust your gut feel. Don't sign for that package. Tell the FedEx courier man he has the wrong door. It is success coffee beans you are waiting for not failure. Only unpack failure. Interrogate every idea that comes into your life, every relationship. What is the aroma around it? If it smells like success it probably is success. Daily you have to find things that connect you to your moment of success and they are embedded in everything you do. Everything you touch has an aroma to it, discern it: you will soon train your senses to pick up that whiff in the air, and act accordingly. Distinguish success from failure. There's an energy to it, an aroma.

Let me unpack this further: in every demand supply chain there is point of equilibrium, this is what we call the moment of success. Success happens weeks or days long before it manifest in the physical. Smell it means set up things that can help you stay inspired for a s long as you can Smelling it means imagine that every phone call or email will eventual lead you to that connection you need. But more than that you can smell success in the air. You are not ten steps away from the realisation of your dream but you are just one step away. Anything can happen any moment from now. You eat food that reminds you of who you are and every challenge you see an opportunity to show you are strong and display your changed mind-set.

When you do that, it means: you are smelling success it. It is here and you can't wait to wake up because the next day bring a greater opportunity. To manifest the power within you. Your breakthrough has finally come and you are in no position to join the company of doubter your mind has been set that this is your chance to blossom. You've come this far and all that you have gone through has created a way for you to discern when your moment has come. You can smell it and this has nothing to do with waiting for something to happen first but you choose to believe this.

Over the years I have seen friend, family and church members failing to possess their possession because they could not smell it in the air and they were not ready when the chance showed up. They refused to do their part. Success is by association and so by smelling it means that you also acknowledge that your network is your net worth. You are not just flying by yourself to some lone island. No, you are on a journey with a whole lot of people on your side willingly will show up and be of assistance to you in times of need because your success is their success and their success is your success too!

Someone once said: freeways are not for free. I believe it was a gentleman called Zwelinzima Vavi, a refined Unionist who was at the helm of Cosatu, a labour federation union back in South Africa. I have a saying of my own to share with you. Are you ready? Pause for a moment: this might just change how you see aviation and wealth, completely.

Flying economy is not economical. Flying economy class might one day turn out to be the most economically uneconomic – and foolish – decision you have ever made. Period. Why? I am glad you asked. See, to smell wealth and mega success, you have to be in the presence of success and great wealth. You do not wake up one morning and smell coffee in your house, unless it is nearby brewing in the kitchen. All those times you are busy trying to save money flying economy class, what are you doing? You are putting a curtain between you and success. You are putting yourself further away from the type of network that can totally shift your net-worth by many digits. See business class more as an investment in belonging to the right club, a stepping stone towards owning your own private jet.

It's not about the comfort of the cabin it is about who you end up next to. You will overhear and smell success. You will smell success. You will ultimately attain success. Fly fewer times, but fly like a high flyer. Be bold, pick wisely.

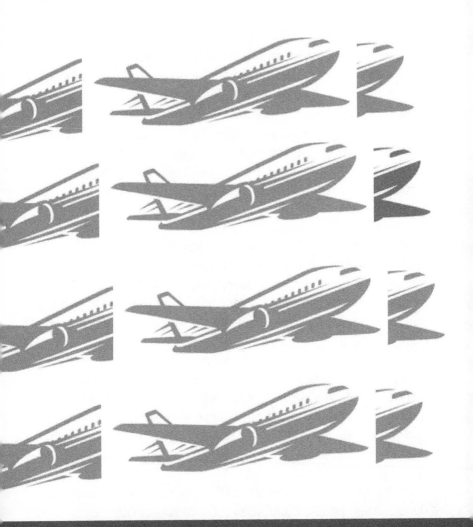

" Flying economy class might one day turn out to be the most economically uneconomic – and foolish – decision you have ever made. Period. Why? To smell wealth and mega success, you have to be in the presence of success and great wealth. It's not about the comfort of the cabin it is about who you end up next to. You will overhear and smell success. You will smell success. You will ultimately attain success. Fly fewer times, but fly like a high flyer. Be bold, pick wisely. "

Let that sink in. What aroma do you bring yourself in contact with? Great wealth leaves aromas that inspires you. When you find yourself being surrounded by broke and brokenness all the time, what will that do to you? Go figure. We have learnt that Tom's suffering caused a suffering to the landlords family and Shop Z but imagine if company A is close friend of Shop Z and they both incentives Company to keep their staff and give them a raise this in turn creates a sustainable winning economy for the whole of Area C.

With us and your team and your people and my people we are building together. You are not alone and you have to understand that we are doing our part every day. For instance me writing this book and getting it into your hands is called me doing my part and you reading this book and putting into practice is you doing your part.

Always keep this in mind: success is a shared experience no wonder most millionaires end with backbiters, haters and naysayers. Those who did not believe in them in the first place and will eventually want to say something negative about what they cannot believe.

I always say that you cannot confirm or stay true to what you doubt. When people doubt the reality of something they cannot prove it exists unless they have changed their doubt into faith or believing in the existence of the same. Once you doubt something your mind is always looking for disproving the reality of the thing so therefore no matter what evidence is brought in you will find an excuse not to believe it. So we want you to focus on your relationships with people.

You need to treat people in such a way that you earn their trust. You have to have a team that trust you and you must trust them. Everyone you have ever had the opportunity to do good to and used it, is like person who has received a deposit from you. People who have a good rapport of you are more likely to take your word and work with you. It is never too late to build a team of people that can share with you in this journey of success.

The power of a good network is in the ideas they share and the level of trust amongst the members. There are many people with followers on Facebook that could never lend them even $10 in times of need. You see those people either do not trust you because they do not know you and they simply do not see any real value in your friendship.

You have to discern not just smell it but discern the kind of people you have around. Because believe it or not show me your friends and will tell you who you are is real.

Conduct a brief inspection of your phone's contact list and take careful note of how many numbers you have stored.

- How many numbers you have stored on your phone?

_____

- How many are worth keeping going forward?

_____

And most importantly: why?

Consumers and businesses need to become more familiar with a concept that comes quite naturally to the wealthy. It is called: number profitability. Put simply, what is the profitability of those numbers you are deciding to store on your phone? Perhaps you had no way of knowing an answer to that question at first, but now, has it been years since you stored a certain contact number? Three things have occurred, quite possibly:

1. You contacted that number or text it, and the results proved non-profitable, socially or economically.
2. You did not contact that number for the last four years.
3. You contacted that number but had no feedback. Why keep it?

Either of the above scenarios are pointing to this: that number or numbers are probably consuming space for a number that is deserving of your time and storage. Make a decision. Bring the same thinking to relationships. There has to be value you derive, and that value has to be a two way street. You must be adding value. Is it time you reach for the delete button? Time to clear the clutter? Time to make way for the good by flushing out the bad? Do the right thing.

Be decisive, be honest and most importantly: be business minded even about your social relations. It's critical.

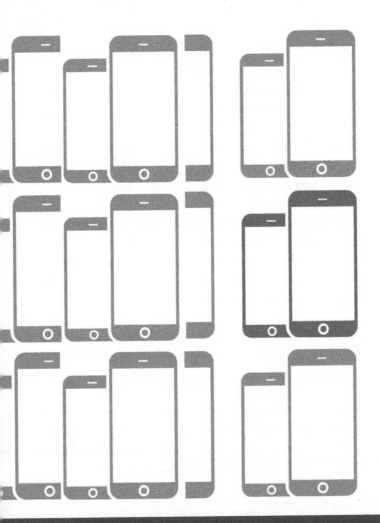

Consumers and businesses need to become more familiar with a concept that comes quite naturally to the wealthy. It is called: number profitability. Put simply, what is the profitability of those numbers you are deciding to store on your phone? Perhaps you had no way of knowing an answer to that question at first, but now, has it been years since you stored a certain contact number? Time to delete?

Each day is a gift. Never forget that. Each day is a God given gift. Why take time in the morning or evening to meditate on these beautiful chances given to by God. Only to proceed to waste them on a contact or network that does not deserve you? You do not want junk in your network or your life. What you want to do is clear friendships in business and personal relationships that are futile. Only leave those that are promising, positive and hold prospects of adding measurable value, fun or profit.

Having written the answers to the above question your mind will become clearer and more precise in determining what company you keep and why. Determining what should define your network, and that ultimately determines your net-worth, make no mistake about that.

With the junk out of the way, you can start building worthwhile networks, bringing yourself in the vicinity of real net-worth enhancing wealth creating opportunities.

Live a life of purpose in everything you do. Your contact list is no different. Live with a real purpose, be on a purpose driven mission, one that benefits you and those in your vicinity. Invite new people into your life, new contacts, and new possibilities.

Some things worth noting:

1. If the quality is good never worry about quantity.
2. You don't need to know everybody, instead you just need to know someone who knows someone who knows Someone who can make things happen.

Change is never without some level of discomfort. That discomfort is sometimes brought about by the sobering questions we need to have with ourselves, the man in the mirror. That type of honesty is necessary. Ready to be honest? Only honesty will do for the next set of questions:

How many contacts do you have on your social media?

_____

Are they useful, beneficial or redundant?

_____

What value are you deriving out of them – do a scan?

_____

_____

_____

What social media platforms do you need to get rid of?

_____

More sobering honest moments:

How many numbers need to be deleted?

_____

How many numbers need to be nurtured?

_____

More action time:

3. Focus on the power of 10 or 20 or 100 good people and ask them to do the same on their network.
4. If we focus on 20 and they do the exact same and teach the follower the same on the fourth time this doubles we would have a network of 160 000 people

in our network, just like that? Or perhaps for you it is
millions of people, later. Great contacts. Not lame ones.

We are all connected worldwide we have to trust that the person
we know knows someone else other than just us.
Plan of action! Choose to build your team of 20.

Your network this is going to be your net-worth.

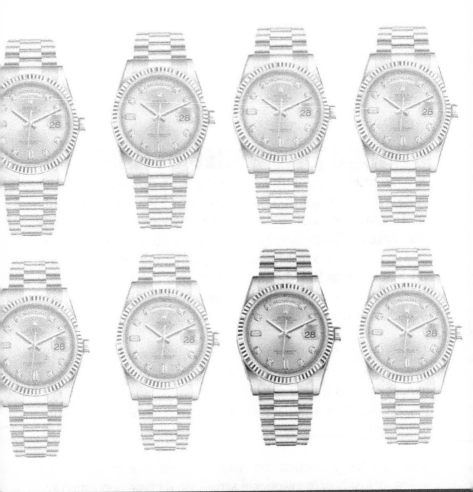

That is as far from the truth as can be. If something is worth doing, it is worth doing right now, right away, not tomorrow. I almost laughed when I came across a poster with a fist raised in the middle. With a declaration across it: Procrastinators unite... tomorrow! Only one thing stopped me from laughing, the cringe on the inside, of just how many people across the 8 billion population live their life like that? Always postponing action due.

How about:

Change your sense of time:

A wise man once said: the people who do not respect or fully grasp the value of time are those who do not really understand or appreciate the worth or value of their life. Interestingly enough those who do not have a great sense of time do not have clarity of vision. Meaning they do not take action because they are deceived to think they will have all the time in the world...someday to act on what is important.

That is as far from the truth as can be. If something is worth doing, it is worth doing right now, right away, not tomorrow. I almost laughed when I came across a poster with a fist raised in the middle. With a declaration across it: Procrastinators unite... tomorrow!

Only one thing stopped me from laughing, the cringe on the inside, of just how many people across the 8 billion population live their life like that. Always postponing action due. Always putting their priorities and dreams on hold. That is one scary reality, but it happens. Don't let it happen to you. Don't join that Procrastinators party, do not vote for it or lead it. It's time for action.

Nothing beats feelings that are followed by actions! This is the true definition of confirmed faith. There is nothing that can stop a man from succeeding when he is already on the journey. My first act on it was when I had to organize meeting and tell people lets pursue the journey of success. Yes that is what I said! Be brave tell the whole world I believe. We have heard that action speak louder than words. We are going to do just that on this in order to achieve what we desire to achieve. Putting this book down means actions unfold. I am asking you to act! Record every single act and date before and after you execute that action.

Organise meetings with people worth meeting. People to share your purpose and dreams with. Like-minded people. People to learn from. Get out there, do not be passive. Certainly do not procrastinate. Some action time:

How many calls am I going to make this week?

_____

Who am I going to call and why (create a full list):

_____

What am I offering them and what do I want from them?

_____

Make Phone-calls, send those texts, & convene meetings.

Create groups of interest on a laptop/notebook:

CONTACT NUMBERS	Folder created?
INDIVIDUALS NAMES	Names consolidated?
GROUP LOCATION	Venue finalised?
PURPOSE	Purpose defined?
REFLECTION NOTES	Reflected?
WHAT DID I LEARN?	Clarity achieved?

That last item is so crucial that it is worth expanding on. Learn something new every day. It's exciting to do.

Daily learning will:

1. Enhance your quality of life. Learning provides you with an escape when you need it, knowledge when you seek it, and a great pastime.
2. Reduce stress. A new hobby can be a great stress reliever. It helps us break out of our normal patterns of behaviour as it gives our brains something to think about other than our daily worries.
3. Gain confidence. When we succeed in learning something we feel better, more confident in ourselves and our ability to tackle all sorts of new tasks.
4. Knowledge is power. When you have knowledge, you have the power to achieve many things. One of the most crucial reasons to learn something new is that you gain power when you do.
5. Improve your mental health. One reason why learning has a positive impact on our mental well-being is that it is often about setting goals or targets and achieving these. This sense of achievement is an important part of 'doing well'.

6. Socialising. Often learning is a social activity and it can help us connect with other people, which is sometimes difficult to do on a meaningful level in today's electronic world. Social connections are vital to our mental well-being.
7. Be selfish. Learning something new might be the excuse you need for some "me time". Time away from work or family. An appointment with yourself. It might just keep you sane.
8. Have fun. Resolving to learn something new is exciting: the world is full of fascinating skills and talents. And the process of discovering them, not just the end result, is enjoyable and rewarding.
9. Set an example. There's nothing that gets children interested like observing their parents expressing excitement about learning. Inspire your kids to want to learn, too. Better still, learn together and share a common interest for life.
10. Rediscover. Many of us have given up on something with were once enthusiastic about in order to focus on a more secure career path. But doesn't it niggle? Wouldn't you like to know if you still have the skill and the passion for your long neglected hobby?

So: make a commitment to yourself, to make daily learning a habit. You have 24 hours given to you as a gift from God, surely you can spare some minutes to grow yourself and your knowledge base.

A new beginning:

Change your assets:

Did that surprise you? Hopefully it did. Think about it: name one person here on earth that is responsible for your future. Please do not say your parents, because that has an expiry date. Please do not say God: that is vague. Even God expects you to get up and assume responsibility. He will help you but expects you to get up and do some real work. You guessed it: you. You must create an asset list. Then get up and do something about ticking those boxes as you gather those assets. If you don't have assets you will probably have debts.

It's time to have the future you want. Time to take it and claw for those inches you have lost. Have you seen the football clip by Al Pachino, pass by Youtube and look it up, it might change your grit, your why and certainly your fight. I was tempted to repeat that speech here, but guess what: put that on your action item, get that speech from Youtube. That locker room moment will shift your perspective on fighting for what you want, and believe.

You have planned, you have applied thought to it, you have reflected, you have gone through the other seven steps. Now it is time for the most critical step. Execution. Time to taste success. True success must be tasted in senses, this means don't just be imaginary but put yourself in a position where you can eat, drink and enjoy success. Food is our daily bread but as to what role it should play in motivation most people never care and they just eat what makes them happy. Meet people closer to places where you like to eat, reward yourself with some cheesecake every time you do well (my wife and I do).

Taste success by first assembling your vision board. Collect photos of what you want. Then focus on those for days to come. Let them inspire and inform your actions. Let them keep you accountable. Let them remind you what is important to you. Pin your dreams onto your wall and stare back at them daily. Do something daily towards the attainment of that which is in front of you.

It was Prentice Mulford 1834 – 1891, author of "Thoughts Are Things" who penned these words:

Whatever the mind is set upon, or whatever it keeps most in view, that it is bringing to it, and the continual thought or imagining must at last take form and shape in the world of seen and tangible things.

Never seek permission to succeed. Next time I land my private jet at an airport somewhere on this planet: I dare you to be the one whose jet is next to mine. **Get out there jet-setter: make it happen!**